JAGUAR DREAM

CLOTHES DON'T MAKE THE MAN

DADASAHEB LANDAGE

Made with ♥ on the Notion Press Platform
www.notionpress.com

To,

My Parents,

Aai and Anna

My lovely daughters

Ariya and Asiya

Contents

FOREWORD

"Hi Dada. Believe it or not, I have only just read "Jaguar Dream". It's an incredible story and makes me want to follow his life story as each dream is realized. It is also very well written. I had a laugh about you stopping mid-journey with your taxi driver for tea. I liked it... and I'm a real critic when it comes to writing."

Mrs. Pauline Stephens Petty

A 73-year-old lady I met in Nassau, Bahamas, she is a retired Shell Bahamas management executive.

Preface

You can't predict who's your next mentor. They say, "Appearances can be deceptive", and that is so true. This short story is about how and why I made some assumptions about a person who made brief appearance in my life and how I was lucky enough to correct myself to further strengthen my belief in the very quote.

Many a times, we make false assumptions and impressions about people in our lives. We fail to realise that each one of us, fight our own distinct battles in the journey called life, and everyone has a story to tell. So, learn to respond instead of reacting to situations or people. Don't be judgmental. Be kind. Be that memorable person in someone's life who creates a positive vibe.

One of my friends always greets me, how's life treating you man? instead of asking, how are you? And I feel, he's so right. In this world, we don't live life, life treats us. Life never happens the way we plan it. There are always surprises and one must be ready to face them. So, remain motivated and enjoy the journey of this beautiful life.

ACKNOWLEDGEMENTS

I would like to express my deepest gratitude and appreciation to the many people who made this book possible.

My wife *Kavita* for constantly supporting my ideas and making sure I remain motivated all the time.

My 10-year-old daughter *Ariya* who read the book draft and stamped "Pappa! It's nice," the biggest compliment for me.

Namresh my ex-colleague and a long-distance friend for making time to talk on various topics, review my write-ups and give feedback. He's in Sydney, Australia. We only met once in last 8 years, but the bond is the strongest. Thanks mate.

My colleague *Snehal Majale*, for reading my drafts and encouraging me to do more. Thanks for being there pal, I will keep coming to you for more opinions.

My running mate Pradeep Lomte, who studied the draft and discussed in detail and said, “It was like a running a half marathon together, pure joy!” Haha!! Thanks for invaluable feedback Pradeep.

And finally, thanks Notion press for building easy to use online self-publishing platform. Keep up the good work team.

Prologue

I managed to correct myself.

So, why I chose this story to be my very first book when I had numerous other narratives? The answer was easy. It's simple, inspiring, thought instilling and I believed that the readers would relate it to themselves. So, I'm confident that all of us will recount this story to at least one incident from the past. For it's so very common to fall prey to negative human emotions and act.

15th Jan 2021

"You never get a second chance to make a first impression." ~ Will Rogers.

I reached Mumbai at 10:30 in the night after almost 18 hours of travel from Brunei. Brunei to Coimbatore and Coimbatore to Mumbai with 5 hours of transit. It was definitely the longest travel I've ever done at a single stretch. I still had another 4-5 hours of cab travel to home - Pune. Body and mind were pretty much fatigued, I was looking forward to see my family and much needed sleep at home.

I collected my baggage, came out of the airport, and called the cab driver. To my surprise, he said, he's still on his way. I expected him to be waiting at the terminal entrance. He asked me to come to the level 4 parking.

I was not very happy as I had informed the cab agency about my exact arrival time. It took me 10-15 minutes to reach level 4 parking. The elevator queues were longer than ever I thought.

One of my friends work at the Mumbai airport, I tried to call him to see if he's working in late shift. Can meet him briefly, I thought. But he didn't answer the phone.

I called the driver again and informed that I've reached. He asked me to wait for some more time. It was 10:45 in the night. My body and mind had started giving in to the night and travel exhaustion. I was not impressed by the cab driver and my voice did express it to some extent. I tried not to be rude.

After waiting for about 10 minutes. Someone approached me.

The guy looked uglier. Aged between 20-25. Full grown beard, much like Tom Hanks of Castaway, shirt and jeans needed wash badly, a scarf converted into a mask? no shoes, just a pair of purpose serving sandals, lean and weak body.

Oh no!! I was scared. What about hygiene? How can someone present themselves like this at an international airport? Can someone be so uncaring when the entire world is wrapped up in a series of Covid-19 waves? I couldn't believe myself going with this guy on a 4-hour journey ahead, but what option I had? It was 11 PM. To be fair, on any other day, I could have tried to get a new cab using airport taxi service, but have I had the strength to leave level 4 parking, walk back with luggage, wait again in elevator queues, and book a new one? I sank. Moreover, I can't reject anyone on the face, it's just too rude for me.

He asked me to give my trolley of bags to him. I was going to say, "No it's ok I'll carry," but ended up handing it over to him reluctantly. I couldn't speak a word but just walk behind him to the car. He kept my bags in the boot space. We moved into the car, fortunately he had the sanitizer inside. He used it and offered me the same, I said, "don't worry, I have my own."

I took my sanitizer out and rubbed to my hands, palms.

2

I pondered over this unpleasant and "unprofessional" driver. People like him can never do anything good for the society. How can he be so irresponsible during such pandemic times? What it takes to keep yourself clean and a little presentable? Is he even sparsely worried about his own health and others? He doesn't belong to this profession. He can never be successful at it.

He paid for the parking and drove out of airport parking. He tried to ask a few questions, and I kept my answers very very short. I didn't feel like talking to this ugly looking guy.

My chain of thoughts didn't break. I wondered why in the heaven's name cab agency provided me with such a driver. I wanted to complain this to my company HR, so I picked up my phone to send a text but something inside me said, don't do it, so I just checked my messages and few other things. I kept my phone aside and tried to sleep.

I generally try to speak to the drivers so that the travel doesn't become boring. But today I didn't feel like talking.

ꕥ

3

At one of the junctions, he tried to cross traffic lights just before it turned red and got stuck in the middle of the road. Everybody started cursing him. I was annoyed. Mumbai it was hundreds of vehicles even at midnight. He took a reverse and managed to make way for traffic coming from the right side. The driver looked undisciplined.

I was looking out of the car window, not much has changed in last 10 months except for a few flyovers, road works and new diversions, I thought to myself.

ᐊ

4

I heard a local train crossing parallelly, I saw nothing but the lit windows of the train-cars in the dark. They say it's the lifeline of this city. Mumbai is amazing, all commute options available at any time of the day and night.

The car stopped. Traffic jam? All traffic lanes moved slowly. We had reached to a toll plaza and there were long lines. I was surprised as it was around mid-night.

"Which place is this?" I broke my silence involuntarily.

"Vashi," the driver answered.

"Ok, but why so many vehicles at this time around?" I expressed my curiosity.

"It's normal at this time, this is Mumbai, Sir. ", He said.

"Oh! Maybe I don't know. I never traveled at this time through Mumbai.," I clarified.

"Keep wearing mask, you may see a few police personnel and they charge a fine if they see us without masks," He added.

The guy sounded friendly.

We crossed the toll station.

I used my sanitizer again.

Silence again. He kept driving.

We were in the cab for more than an hour, and still hadn't crossed Panvel, far end of the Mumbai.

Mumbai gives me a different feel every time I come here. It's a different world altogether.

Due to a flyover work, he took a diversion and passed through a very narrow lane which took us to BKC, Bandra Kurla complex, one of the poshest areas in Mumbai with huge skyscrapers of most corporates. I was amazed to see new Reliance global building and few other corporate houses.

I tried a take video of the dazzling Mumbai night.

I was disturbed as the cab stopped again. Some kids were riding electric bikes and one of them had fallen. Some folks helped them and cleared the road. Even kids don't sleep at midnight in Mumbai. Crazy! I thought, but that's the story of every big Indian city, isn't it? I asked myself.

We moved ahead.

We crossed Panvel finally, out of Mumbai and hit Express way.

ﻌ

Break that ice!

It was dark outside, nothing to see except for passing vehicles. The silence in the cab had grown. It made me uneasy. I was going against my nature. I loved talking to people. If I'm with someone, I can't be silenced.

I tried to trigger a conversation.

I asked driver if the cab belonged to him. He proudly said,

"Yes Sir! I also have another cab and I've employed another driver on it," He explained himself briefly.

I was impressed and that made me ask another question.

"How long have you been driving?"

"3 years. I was driving for another cab agency for a year or so and bought my first car after that. And within one year, I bought one more car. I have a dream of owning 10 sedan cars like this and a *Jaguar* with yellow plate.", He completed.

Hired cars are yellow plated in India. So, Jaguar for hire.

I was stunned!! What's this ugly looking guy talking about?

My heart melted. Suddenly the ugly looking guy had turned into a respectable entrepreneur. I felt privileged to be in his company.

My curiosity grown.

"Where are you from and what are your parents?" I asked.

"Chakan, I'm from Chakan. My mother works in a factory in Chakan, Pune and father is a security guard."

"How old are you?"

"I'm 27. "

"Married? "

"Not yet, but I'm planning to get married only after 2-3 years. By that time, I will have at least 5 cars and I'll be earning 5 times of what I earn Today."

He was super confident. I never see such self-assurance in most strugglers, and this was extra-ordinary.

"I'm impressed by your dream and planning. Congratulations and all the best!! Dreaming such a thing itself is a huge feat. Just don't give up and it will come true one day.", I said.

"You are right Sir. There's no question of giving up after I've reached so far. There was a day when me and family had very tough times. My father had undergone angioplasty and we had a loan of 80k. I was not earning enough. I remember the days when I slept eating peanuts for dinner. I've also seen a day when I felt like committing suicide. I've overcome those days, so no question of going back and giving up. I don't have no shame of doing hard work. This is my 3rd Pune -Mumbai trip in the day and I'm not tired. My dream keeps me awake.," He replied.

He talked profoundly.

My heart filled with compassion, and it wished all the success to this dream pursuer.

I said, "Take care of your health. Health is everything, you can lose and earn back everything, but not health. So, do take proper rest and have healthy food habits in the pursuit of dream."

"I play cricket with my friends whenever I get time," he responded positively.

"Ok good.," I tried to keep the conversation going.

But there's a lot of competition in this business, I hear a lot about it from my company transport vendors and cab drivers. Do you feel scared?

"I've studied this business and I know precisely which vehicle gives how much revenue. From cars to trucks and buses, I know everything," He continued.

"I've accepted loss making offers, just to understand and learn intricacies of this business. And I'm not scared, because I'm competing with myself," He finished.

"That's so good, yes, you need to learn small things about business if you want to grow big," I said.

6

We stopped for a tea break at a food plaza. The time was 1.30 AM.

I love these expressway food plazas. Express way has quite a few of them. These bustling food malls serve almost every Indian dish and host western fast-food chains and cafes.

I was not feeling sleepy now. The driver's talk was not less than a motivational speaker's talking.

The food court was a little crowded by night travelers. I preferred a tea vendor who had less people at the counter. We finished our tea and got back in the car. I used sanitizer.

We continued our journey.

Don’t let other folks tell you what you could do, instead trust your sensitivity, and get ahead.

I kept thinking about this driver. I asked,

“What made you think about starting this business?”

He continued, "I was doing a newspaper distribution job when I was in school and that’s when I was attracted to earning money. I didn’t like school and was dropped off. I didn’t rejoin school."

"I started working in a factory. Did that for a few years. I learnt driving and I liked it. While I was at the factory, I managed bills of all vendors which included transport vendors too. That’s how I understood about how the transport business operates and I felt transport will be good for me."

"One of my friends bought a car and started this business. I told him, I’ll buy a car too, but in return he said, you cannot buy a car and even if you buy, you cannot survive. He treated me as if I was a rat."

"That incident is carved in my heart and ignited a fire in me. Today my friend has the same car, and I‘m the owner of two cars. I don’t want to compete with him but I’m thankful to him for not believing in me."

The driver opened his heart to me.

"That's good. Was your business impacted by Covid-19 ?" I asked.

"Yes, but fortunately after initial few months, I started Pune-Mumbai trips and I survived."

"I'm also investing in mutual funds and expecting a few 20-30 lakhs (2-3 million) in there in next 5 years. I'm planning a fixed monthly saving for my kids."

He had so much to say.

Hardships make us strong. Problems give birth to wisdom.

Clearly, he learnt from his past and was trying take his life to a whole different level.

"Planning for kids before marriage?" I smiled.

"Your, "would be" wife will be glad to hear this." I said and laughed.

"But I'm happy that, you are very clear about what you want to do to make your future bright. Keep it up!!" I repeated.

ꕥ

This was the same person who wanted to end his life for a paltry loan of 80 thousand and some hardships, today he's talking about lakhs (Hundred thousand). Such a transition!! Life changes for better, even better always.

Hardships change persons. I was witnessing the positive one.

He got a call from one of his cricketing friends. They had won a night cricket tournament and wanted this driver to pick them up. He asked them to wait until he drops me home.

I said, "what's your background? Do you have any property? I mean land."

"No, nothing. It's a start from zero for me and I'm very happy. I'm enjoying the journey." The driver said.

I had truly learnt something new. Never had I met such a cab driver in all these years of my travel. So inspiring and self-motivated.

By the time I reached home, I had decided that I would give him a good tip. He dropped me. I offered him 100 bucks and his eyes blinked. He thanked me.

I wished him success for his future journey again.

I couldn't believe my own journey from hesitant to speak to offering a good tip to him. Last 4 hours had supplemented a notable chapter in my life, it started from the quote

"Two things remain irretrievable: time and a first impression." by Cynthia Ozick,

and ended with

"First impression is unfair, because a first impression of somebody is guarded, and you don't know the person." by Frank Oz.

What if I had managed to sleep for 4 hours? I laugh today.

ꙮ

Every incident leaves us with some life changing values and philosophies. I could gather some of them when working on this book.

- Best of the things come from within us. If the desire is stronger enough, success happen to you.
- All you need is a desire to grow and achieve, means come to you if take a step.
- Only you can change the course of your life, no one else.
- Remember, life treats us in its own way. So, remain motivated and enjoy the journey of life.
- There are no replacements to hard work and consistency.
- Life changes for better, always.
- Take care of your health as that's your only and real asset.
- Don't shy away from work because you must work hard to transform your life.

A startling revelation...

Don't let individuals tell you what you could do, instead trust your sensitivity, and get ahead, outcomes will follow.

How's the driver doing now?

When I decided to publish this story as a book, the first thought came to my mind was to find out how the driver is doing now. I knew, readers will be curious to know the current status of his plans and possibly follow his life story as it unfolded. Did his life shape the way he wanted and had planned? Did he give up? Or he managed to remain inspired, disciplined and achieved greater heights as he had wished and visualized?

I have had my fears. I wanted to learn only positives about the main character of this story. My mind was not ready to accept any diversion or U turn in his life. My weakness!! My heart had only wished a better life and progress for him. I didn't try to contact him even though it is possible in this closely knit world. A feared human I am.

And then, the only reason I authored this story was because, the person briefly appeared in my life and made me understand the importance of taking a moment to pause before "labelling" people in our lives. And I was impressed by his self-inspired expedition. Therefore, the story must end with another realization, "This is how a part of inspired life looked like."

What my friends and well-wishers had to say,

Snehal Majale

"Very often we judge a book by its' cover.. even though we know it's not right.. but unfortunately in the current world we cannot trust people very easily.. you were fortunate that you got the time and opportunity to revise your judgement of the person.. not everyone gets this chance.. write up is good, interesting actually.."

Namresh Pimple

"Cool yaar, people can be so amazing.." Story is pretty good, It's a simple tale, writing is in accordance, right flow, changes in the story happening at the right times, and not too long. And obviously does have the content to keep you interested.."

Printed by Libri Plureos GmbH in Hamburg, Germany